DR. BOB'S
AMAZING WORLD OF
ANIMALS
PUMAS

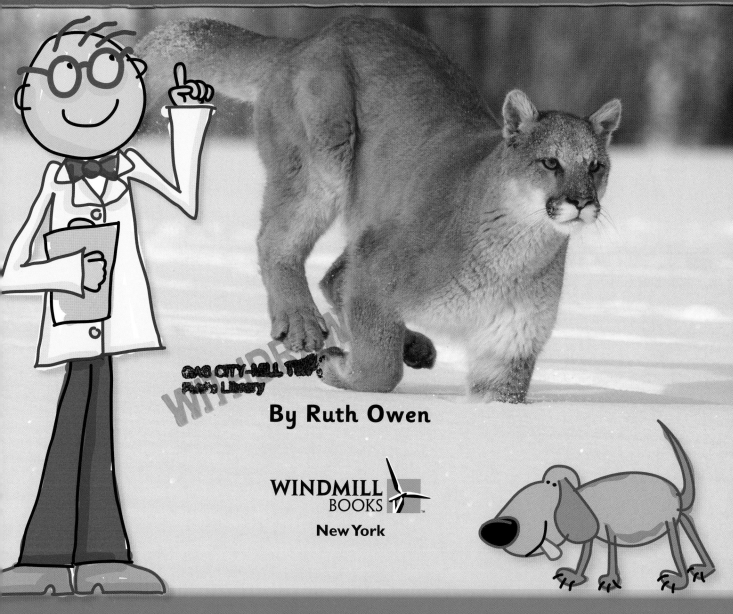

By Ruth Owen

WINDMILL BOOKS
New York

Published in 2014 by Windmill Books, An Imprint of Rosen Publishing
29 East 21st Street, New York, NY 10010

Editor for Ruby Tuesday Books Ltd: Mark J. Sachner
US Editor: Joshua Shadowens
Designer: Trudi Webb

Photo Credits: Cover, 1, 4–5, 7, 9, 10–11, 12–13, 14–15,
16–17, 18–19, 20–21, 22–23, 24–25, 26–27, 28–29, 30 © Shutterstock.

Library of Congress Cataloging-in-Publication Data

Owen, Ruth, 1967–
 Pumas / by Ruth Owen.
    pages cm. — (Dr. Bob's amazing world of animals)
 Includes index.
 ISBN 978-1-47779-032-8 (library) — ISBN 978-1-47779-033-5 (pbk.) —
 ISBN 978-1-47779-034-2 (6-pack)
 1. Puma—Juvenile literature. I. Title.
 QL737.C23O945 2014
 599.75'24—dc23
                                        2013028183
Manufactured in the United States of America

CPSIA Compliance Information: Batch #BW14WM: For Further Information contact Windmill Books, New York, New York at 1-866-478-0556

Contents

The Puma

Welcome to my amazing world of animals. Today, we are visiting **wilderness** areas in North and South America to find out about pumas.

Let's investigate...

Hank's
WOOF OF WISDOM!

Pumas are members of the cat family. This animal group includes tigers, lions, leopards, cheetahs, and even pet cats.

Pumas are also known as mountain lions, cougars, panthers, and catamounts. This cat has many different names, but it is just one **species** of animal.

A puma

Pumas are very shy animals.
It is unusual to see one in the wild.

Land of the Puma

Pumas live in many different **habitats**, from forests in Canada to swamps in Florida.

The orange areas on the map are where pumas are found.

Some pumas live in deserts, while others live on the slopes of mountains.

A puma searches the area for signs of prey.

Pumas prefer to live in areas where there are lots of rocks or thick bushes and trees. In these areas, there are plenty of places for the large hunters to stay hidden as they creep up on **prey**.

A Puma's Territory

Adult pumas live alone. Each puma has a **territory**, or home area, where it hunts.

A territory may be an area just 3 miles (5 km) wide. The territory may also be much larger, perhaps 10 miles (16 km) wide by 30 miles (48 km) long.

The territories of female pumas sometimes overlap. Males, however, don't usually share their neighborhood with any other males.

Hank's
WOOF OF WISDOM!

Pumas send messages to each other by making scratch marks on trees and logs. They also send messages in their urine and waste.

My territory stay away!

A male puma's large territory may include the smaller territories of several females.

A puma scratching a tree

Puma Bodies

Adult pumas have furry coats that come in gray, pale brown, dark brown, or reddish-orange.

A puma's back legs are longer than its front legs. This helps the cat when it is running and jumping.

Puma Size Chart

Adult male puma

Weight
adult male =
115 to 230 pounds
(52–104 kg)

An adult puma's head and body can
be up to 5 feet (1.5 m) long.

A puma's tail
measures up
to 33 inches
(84 cm) long.

Adult female puma

Weight
adult female =
60 to 140 pounds
(27–64 kg)

Puma Skills

Pumas are highly athletic cats that can run, swim, make huge jumps, and climb trees with ease.

A puma can jump 20 feet (6.1 m) up a mountainside. That's as high as jumping onto the roof of a two-story building!

A young puma running

If wild dogs or a pack of wolves come close to a puma, the cat escapes these enemies by climbing up a tree.

These powerful cats can also easily leap 18 feet (5.5 m) from the ground into the branches of a tree.

What's on the Menu?

Like all members of the cat family, pumas are **predators**, which means they hunt other animals for food.

Pumas hunt large animals such as deer, moose, elk, caribou, and sheep.

White-tailed deer

They also catch and eat smaller creatures, including coyotes, wild pigs, beavers, raccoons, skunks, rabbits, squirrels, and birds.

A puma watching prey

Pumas aren't afraid of catching and eating a porcupine. They happily crunch into this prickly prey and even eat the porcupine's quills!

A porcupine

Hunting Tactics

Adult pumas hunt alone during the night, or at dawn and dusk. They use stealth and power to catch their prey.

Once a puma spots a meal, it creeps closer. If the animal is moving, the puma **stalks** its prey staying hidden at all times.

A puma stalking prey

When the puma is just two or three huge leaps away from its prey, it makes a sudden, speedy attack.

The moment of attack!

The puma pounces on its victim from behind. Then it bites into the other animal's neck and drags it to the ground.

A Puma's Dinner

A puma's powerful front legs and paws are designed for grabbing prey. Its strong jaws and long canine teeth are perfect for clamping onto prey when making a kill.

A puma will eat some of the meat it has caught.
Then it hides the rest by covering it with leaves or soil.

Canine teeth

Once its meal is safely hidden, the puma can come
back to feed whenever it is hungry. A large animal
will give the puma food for several days.

A New Family

When it is time to **mate**, a male and female puma meet up. After mating, the two pumas go back to living alone. Male pumas do not help raise their babies.

About three months after mating, a female puma is ready to give birth.

Male puma

Female puma

A female puma chooses a quiet, safe place, such as inside a cave or under a fallen tree, to be her birthing den.

Female puma

Den

In the den, the puma cubs, or kittens, are born. Most females give birth to three or four cubs at one time.

The Puma Cubs

Inside the birthing den, the newborn puma cubs are safe from predators such as bears, wolves, or male pumas that sometimes harm cubs.

This puma cub is just a few days old.

The newborn cubs' eyes are closed, and their fur is covered with dark spots.

The cubs feed on milk from their mother's body.

This cub is a few weeks old.

By the time they are two weeks old, the cubs' eyes have opened.

Hank's
WOOF OF WISDOM!

The cubs' spotted fur makes it harder for predators to see them in long grass and other hiding places.

New Things to Try!

When the puma cubs are about six weeks old, they start eating meat brought to them by their mother.

From about eight weeks old, the cubs leave the den. They follow their mother to the places where she has hidden food. Here, the cubs feed on prey killed by their mother.

Time to explore!

Climbing trees is harder than it looks!

Puma cubs drink their mother's milk until they are about three months old.

A young puma

Growing Up

As the puma cubs grow up, the mother puma teaches them how to stalk and catch their own prey.

When they are about one and a half years old, each cub is ready to leave its mother and live on its own.

Young male pumas begin looking for a mate when they are about three years old.

Cub

A young female puma is ready to have cubs of her own when she is about two and a half years old.

Mother puma

The Future for Pumas

At this moment in time, pumas are not in danger. The future may be difficult for these large, wild cats, however.

The habitats where pumas live are disappearing fast as people build towns, factories, malls, and highways.

Hank's WOOF OF WISDOM!

Pumas often have to cross roads as they walk through their territories. Many are killed by cars and trucks.

It's important that wilderness areas are not destroyed. Then pumas, their prey, and many other species of animals and plants will have wild places to live.

Glossary

habitats (HA-buh-tats) Places where animals or plants normally live. A habitat may be a forest, the ocean, or a backyard.

mate (MAYT) To get together to produce young. Also, the word for an animal's partner with which it has young.

predators (PREH-duh-turz) Animals that hunt and kill other animals for food.

prey (PRAY) An animal that is hunted by another animal as food.

species (SPEE-sheez) One type of living thing. The members of a species look alike and can produce young together.

stalks (STOKS) Follows without being seen.

territory (TER-uh-tor-ee) The area where an animal lives, finds its food, and finds partners for mating.

wilderness (WIL-dur-nis) A wild place where no humans live, such as a desert, forest, or on the slopes of a mountain.

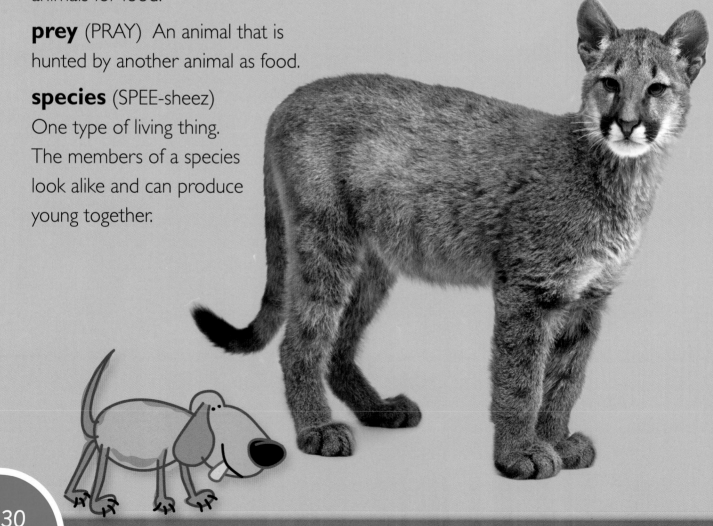

Dr. Bob's Fast Fact Board

A puma cub weighs less than 1 pound (0.5 kg) when it is born.

Pumas communicate using purrs, meows, hissing and spitting, growling, and scream-like noises.

Most wild pumas live for up to 12 years. Pumas in zoos can live for longer, reaching ages of 20 years.

People often think that pumas might attack them when they are hiking or camping. The truth is that these animals are usually afraid of people and just want to be left alone.

Websites

For web resources related to the subject of this book, go to:

www.windmillbooks.com/weblinks

and select this book's title.

Read More

Karlin, Wade. *Pumas*. Killer Cats. New York: Gareth Stevens Weekly Readers, 2012.

Magby, Meryl. *Mountain Lions*. American Animals. New York: PowerKids Press, 2013.

Shores, Erika L. *Mountain Lions*. Wildcats. Mankato, MN: Capstone Press, 2011.

Index